Treasures

A Reading/Language Arts Program

Macmillan
McGraw-Hill

Contributors

Time Magazine, Accelerated Reader

RFB&D 🎧
learning through listening

Students with print disabilities may be eligible to obtain an accessible, audio version of the pupil edition of this textbook. Please call Recording for the Blind & Dyslexic at 1-800-221-4792 for complete information.

A

The McGraw·Hill Companies

**Macmillan
McGraw-Hill**

Published by Macmillan/McGraw-Hill, of McGraw-Hill Education, a division of The McGraw-Hill Companies, Inc., Two Penn Plaza, New York, New York 10121.

Printed in the United States of America

ISBN-13: 978-0-02-198805-1/1, Bk. 2
ISBN-10: 0-02-198805-6/1, Bk. 2
7 8 9 (RJE/LEH) 11

Treasures

A Reading/Language Arts Program

Program Authors

Donald R. Bear
Janice A. Dole
Jana Echevarria
Jan E. Hasbrouck
Scott G. Paris
Timothy Shanahan
Josefina V. Tinajero

Macmillan
McGraw-Hill

Unit 2
Outside My Door

Test Strategy: Right There

Talk About It

How are animal families like our families?

LOG ON Find out more about animal families at **www.macmillanmh.com**

Animal Families

Words to Know

one
her
two
they
does

---

fr<u>o</u>g
h<u>o</u>p
r<u>o</u>ck

Read to Find Out

What do frogs
like to do?

One Frog, Two Frogs

by Lucy Paris

One little frog likes to jump.
Look at **her** hop!

Two little frogs like to sit.
They sit on a rock.

One little frog likes to look.
What **does** she see?

Two little frogs like to play.
Will they play with me?

Genre
Nonfiction gives information about a topic.

Summary

STRATEGY SKILL ✓

Main Idea and Details
As you read, use your **Main Idea and Details Web.**

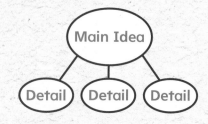

Read to Find Out
What do animal moms and dads do?

Animal
Moms and Dads

by Jose Ramos

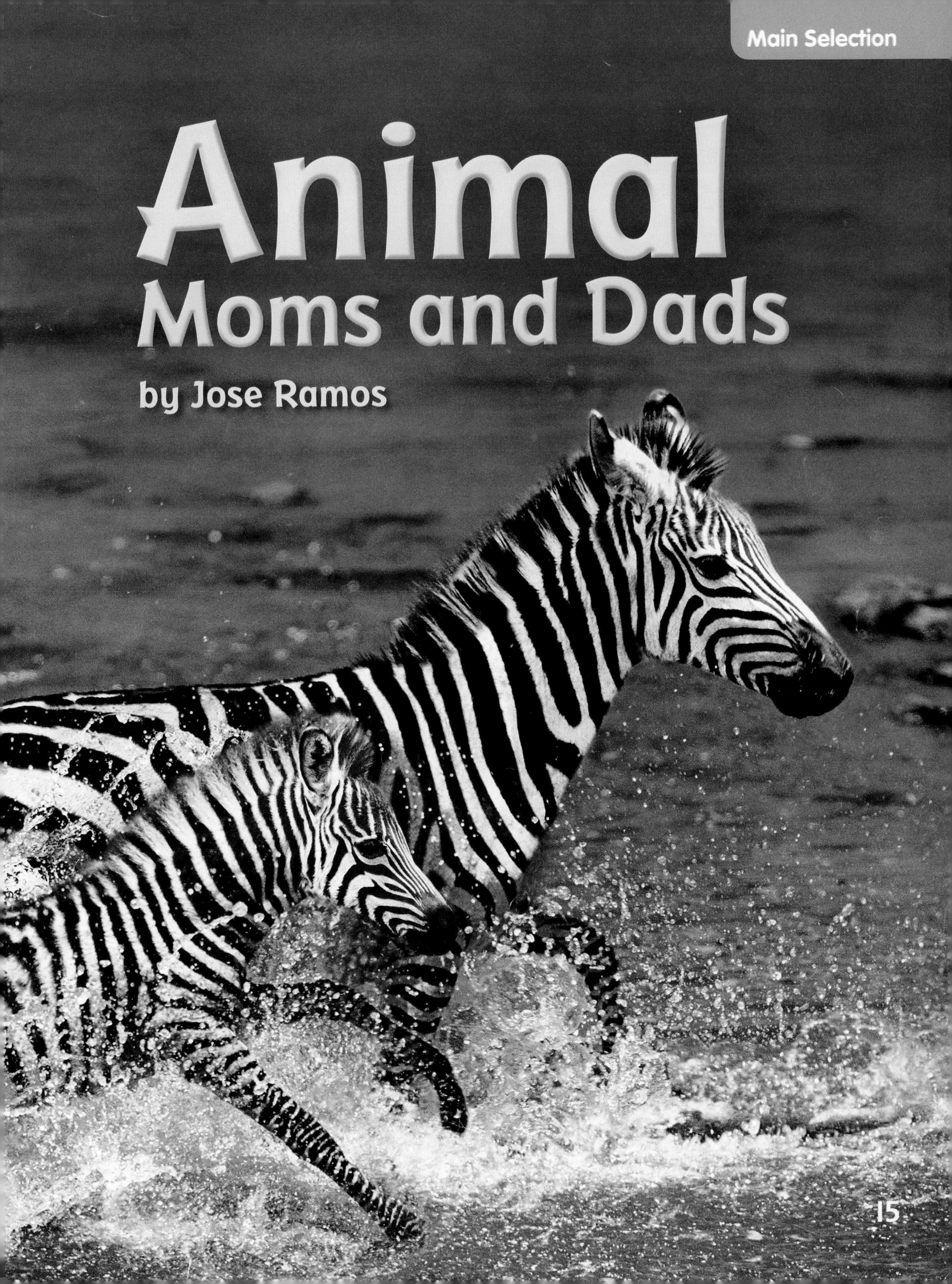

What do animal moms do?
This mom **does** a lot.

What do animal dads do?
This dad does a lot, too.

This mom has food.
Her baby can grab it.

This dad brings food for **two**.
Dad and baby like it a lot!

This mom licks.
Now her baby is soft.

This baby sits with Dad.
Dad will pick off bugs.

This baby is in Mom's sack.
They will hop, hop, hop.

This dad has a big back.
His baby is on top.

See what this mom and dad did.
It was a big job!

Can you see **one** baby?
Can you see two?

What can animal moms and dads do?

They can play, too!

Meet Jose Ramos

Jose Ramos says, "When I was young, my dad took me to the zoo. I wanted to take a photo of every monkey I saw! Today, I'm a dad. I take my kids to the zoo. We take pictures of our favorite animals."

Author's Purpose

Jose Ramos wanted the reader to learn about animals. Draw an animal with its mom and dad. Write about it.

LOG ON Find out more about Jose Ramos at **www.macmillanmh.com**

Comprehension Check

Retell the Selection

Use the Retelling Cards to retell the selection.

Retelling Cards

Think and Compare

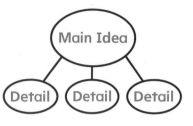

STRATEGY SKILL

1. How do animal moms and dads take care of their babies?

2. How do the grownups in your family take care of you?

3. How do other animals you know take care of their babies?

4. How is *Animal Moms and Dads* like "One Frog, Two Frogs"? How is it different?

Poetry

Genre

In a **Poem**, words are often put together so that they are fun to say.

Literary Element

Rhythmic Patterns are sounds and words that repeat. These give the poem a certain beat.

Find out more about animal families at **www.macmillanmh.com**

Over in the Meadow

An Old Counting Rhyme

Over in the meadow,
In the sand in the sun,
Lived an old mother turtle
And her little turtle one.
"Dig," said the mother.
"I dig," said the one.
So they dug all day
In the sand in the sun.

Over in the meadow,
Where the stream runs blue,
Lived an old mother fish
and her little fishes two.

"Swim," said the mother.
"We swim," said the two.
So they swam all day
Where the stream runs blue.

Over in the meadow,
In the wide oak tree,
Lived an old mother owl
And her little owls three.
"Whoo," said the mother.
"Whoo, Whoo" said the three.
So they whooed all night
In the wide oak tree.

Connect and Compare

How are these moms and babies like the parents and babies in *Animal Moms and Dads*? How are they different?

Write About Families

Sam wrote about what some families do.

What Families Do

Families can help each other.

Families can play together.

Your Turn

Think about how your family takes care of you.

Write about how families take care of each other.

Writer's Checklist

- Does my list have a title?

- Do I write about my family?

- Does each sentence have a noun?

Helping Out

Talk About It

How do you help?
What jobs do you
like to do?

LOG ON Find out more about
helping at
www.macmillanmh.com

39

Words to Know

who

no

some

of

eat

---

m<u>e</u>ss

h<u>e</u>lp

g<u>e</u>t

Read to Find Out

Who will help clean up the mess?

40

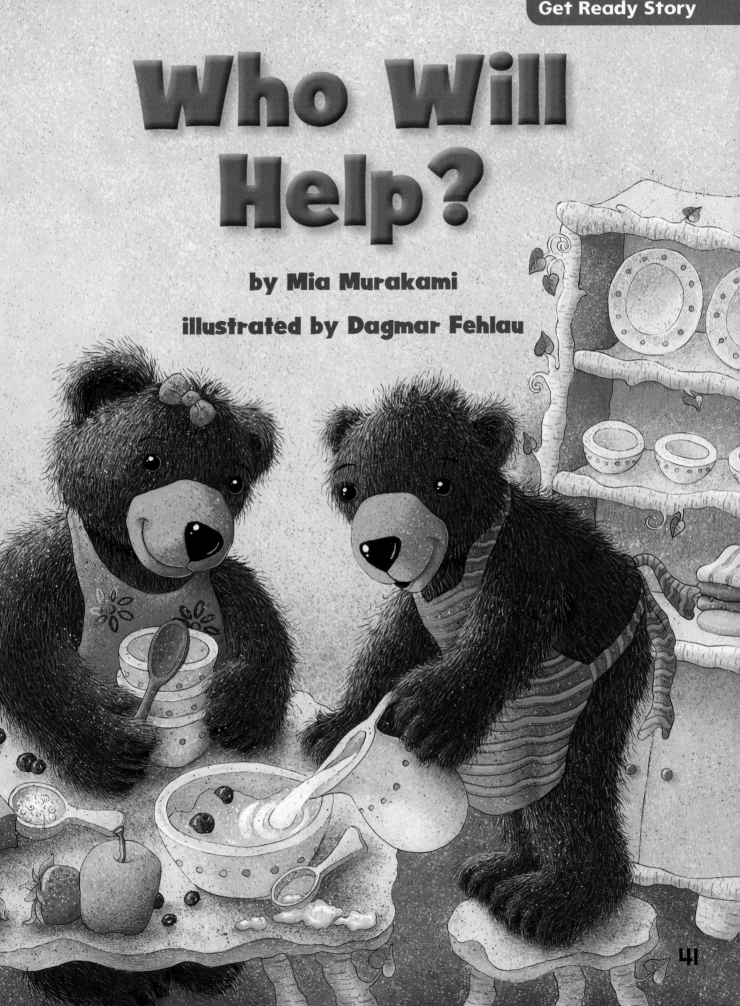

Who Will Help?

by Mia Murakami

illustrated by Dagmar Fehlau

"Look at this mess," said Ben.
"**Who** will help?"

42

"We have **no** mops," said Jen.
"We have no bags," said Tim.

"I will pick up," said Ben.
"I can get **some** **of** it," said Jen.

"I can help, too," said Tim.
"I will **eat** some!"

Comprehension

Genre
A **Folk Tale** is a story that has been told for many years.

Summarize
Retell

As you read, use your **Retelling Chart.**

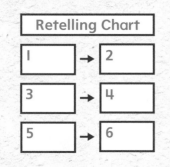

Retelling Chart

1	→	2
3	→	4
5	→	6

Read to Find Out
How does Little Red Hen make bread?

46

Little Red Hen

retold by Cynthia Rothman
illustrated by David Diaz

Award
Winning
Illustrator

Little Red Hen had a bit **of** wheat.
"**Who** will help plant?" said Hen.

"Not I," said Dog.
"Not I," said Pig.
"Not I," said Cat.

"I will go to the well," said Hen.
"Who will help me get **some** water?"

"Not I," said Cat.
"Not I," said Dog.
"Not I," said Pig.

"This is a big job," said Hen.
"Who will help me?"

"Not I," said Cat.
"Not I," said Dog.
"Not I," said Pig.

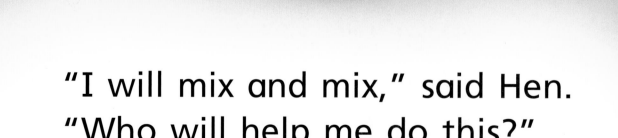

"I will mix and mix," said Hen.
"Who will help me do this?"

"Not I," said Cat.
"Not I," said Dog.
"Not I," said Pig.

"Come quick!" said Hen.
"Look at this bread!"

"This is the best bread," she said.
"Who will help me **eat** some of it?"

"Let me," said Pig.
"Let me," said Cat.
"Let me," said Dog.

"**No**! No!" said Hen.
"This is a job for me!"

David Diaz's Job

David Diaz says, "I remember drawing a face on a worksheet when I was in first grade. I knew then that drawing was what I wanted to do when I grew up."

Other books by David Diaz

LOG ON Find out more about David Diaz at **www.macmillanmh.com**

Illustrator's Purpose

David Diaz drew funny animals. Draw one of the animals. Write about it.

Comprehension Check

Retell the Story

Use the Retelling Cards to retell the story.

Retelling Cards

Think and Compare

Retelling Chart	
1 →	2
3 →	4
5 →	6

1. What does Little Red Hen do with the wheat?

2. What kind of help do you need when you make food?

3. Do you think Little Red Hen should have shared the bread? Tell why or why not.

4. How are Little Red Hen's friends like the bears in "Who Will Help?"

From Wheat to Bread

How does wheat **grow**?
How do we use it?

Seeds

Wheat starts as a little seed.
Farmers plant the seeds.

63

kernels

leaves

stem

roots

A Wheat Plant

The little plants have to get sun.
They have to get water.
They will grow to be big.

Now the wheat is tan.
The farmer picks off the **kernels**.
The kernels are good to eat.

The kernels go to a **factory**.
Here they are crushed.
The little bits of wheat are flour.

We use flour to make bread.
We use it in good things to eat.
That is what we do with wheat!

Connect and Compare

Where does bread come from? Who
helps Little Red Hen make bread?
Who helps make bread in "From
Wheat to Bread"?

Add -*s* to make some nouns name more than one.

How to Make a Snack

Eva wrote about how to make a snack.

How to Make a Snack

1. Get some nuts.

2. Get some grapes.

3. Mix and eat!

Your Turn

Think about a snack you like.

Write a how–to list.

Writer's Checklist

 Are the steps in the right order?

 Do the nouns that mean more than one end with *s*?

 Does each sentence begin with a capital letter?

Where Animals Live

Ants
Go In and Out

Look **into** this ant hill.
Many ants **live** here.

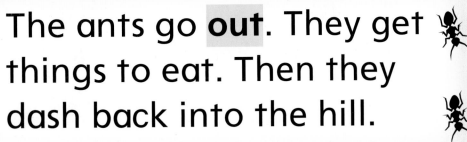

The ants go **out**. They get things to eat. Then they dash back into the hill.

A Prairie Dog Home

Why is this a good home for prairie dogs?

Come meet some prairie dogs. See where they **live**.

This prairie dog lives with **many** prairie dogs.

You can see some of a prairie dog's home.
The rest is under the land.

Prairie dogs dig with big claws. They dig long paths.

Come **into** a prairie dog home.
Can you see where prairie
dogs rest?

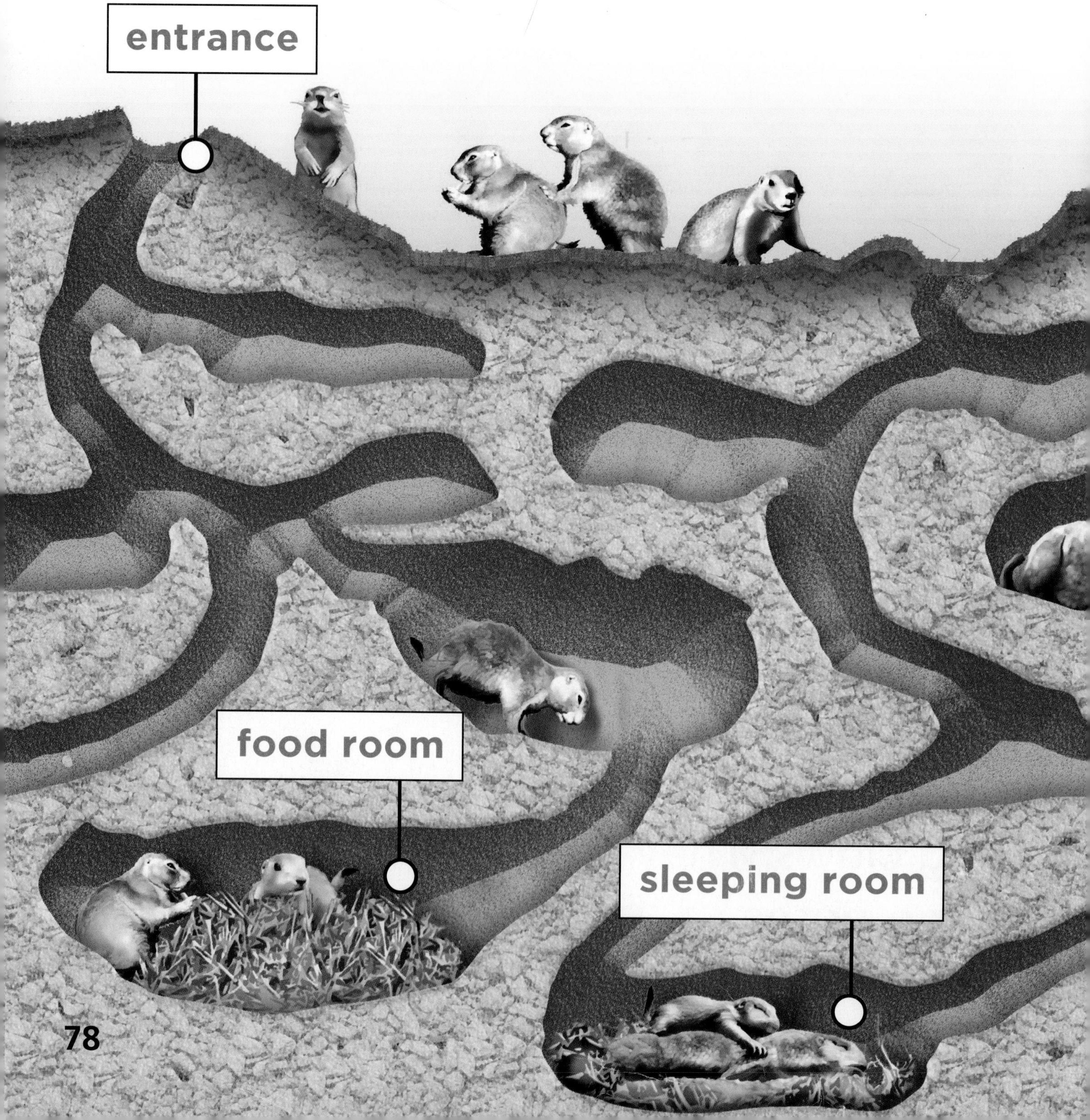

entrance

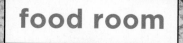

food room

sleeping room

Can you see where prairie dogs have things to eat? Can you see them caring for little prairie dogs?

second entrance

nursery

79

Little prairie dogs come **out** to play. They eat fresh grass. One day they will dig new paths for the prairie dog home.

Comprehension Check

Tell What You Learned

What is a prairie dog home like?

Think and Compare

1. Give three details that show why a prairie dog home is a good home.

2. How is a prairie dog home like your home?

3. Why is underground a good place for some animals to live?

4. How is a prairie dog home like the home in "Ants Go In and Out"?

Test Strategy

Right There
The answer is right there on the page.

READ TOGETHER

A Koala Home

The koala lives in a tree.
It sleeps all day.
It eats lots of leaves.
When it rains, the leaves
make an umbrella.
The koala stays dry.

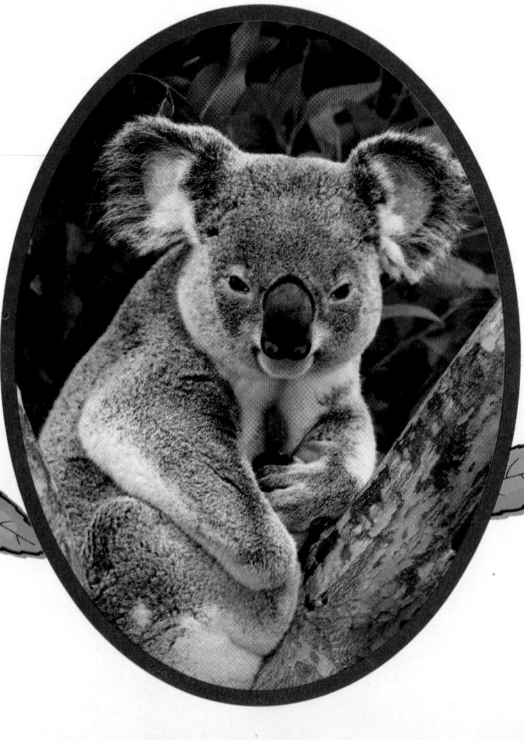

Go On

Directions: Answer the questions.

1. Where do koalas live?

○   ○   ○

2. What do koalas eat?

○   They eat lots of fish.

○   They eat lots of leaves.

○   They eat lots of nuts.

Tip
Look for
key words.

3. What makes an umbrella?

○   ○   ○

 **83**

Write About an Animal Home

Jacob wrote a report about where chipmunks live.

Chipmunks live in holes.

They keep food in their holes.

Your Writing Prompt

Think about an animal and its home. Write a report about this animal's home.

Writer's Checklist

☑ Does my report have details?

☑ Does each sentence begin with a capital letter?

☑ Do my sentences make sense?

Sing and Dance!

Talk About It

When do you sing or dance? What kind of music do you like?

LOG ON Find out more about music at **www.macmillanmh.com**

Words to Know

want
put
show
under
three
make

___

f<u>u</u>n
dr<u>u</u>ms

STRATEGY SKILL

Read to Find Out

What will the fun show be like?

A Fun Show

by Pam Krieger

illustrated by Stacey Schuett

"I **want** to have fun," said Bud.
"We can **put** on a **show**!" said Meg.
"Ruff, ruff," said Pup.

"Come see a show **under** a tent!"
said the kids.
"Ruff, ruff," said Pup.

Meg and Jan sing **three** songs.
Bud plays the drum.
"Ruff, ruff!" sings Pup.

Jack can **make** Pup jump.
It is a fun show!

Comprehension

Genre
Realistic Fiction is a made-up story that could really happen.

Visualize

Retell

As you read, use your **Retelling Chart.**

Retelling Chart	
1 →	2
3 →	4
5 →	6

Read to Find Out
Why is the band fun?

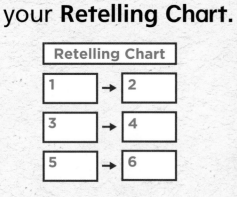

94

The Fun Kids' Band

by Anne Miranda
illustrated by Lynne Cravath

"Aunt Nell, look at that!" said Beth.

"What's the fuss?" asked Aunt Nell.

"It's a band for kids," said Ann.

"We **want** to play in the band!"
said Beth, Bud, Ann, and Will.

"Can the kids play?" asked Aunt Nell.

"Yes!" said a man in a red hat. "I am Gus. **Make** some instruments, kids."

"Make instruments?" asked the kids.

"Yes. Use the things in the box. It is **under** the bandstand," said Gus.

Rap
Tap
Tap

"Look! I can hit this tub," said Bud.
"It sounds just like a drum."
Rap! Tap! Tap!

Hum
Hum
Hum

"Look! I can play the jug," said Ann.
Hum! Hum! Hum!

Crish
Crush
Crash

"Look! I can play the lids!" said Will.
Crish! Crush! Crash!

"What do you want to make, Beth?" asked Aunt Nell.

"I just want to sing," said Beth.

"Can I sing in the **show**?" she asked. "That will be fun for me."

"That will be fun for us, too,"
said the kids.

"Come on," said Will. "Let's play!"

"Now Beth and the band will **put** on a show," said Gus.

"One, two, **three**! Play with me!"

Sing Along with Anne Miranda

Anne Miranda says, "When I was little, I sang in a group with my friend, Elizabeth, her mother, and my neighbor, Cathy, who was in high school. Once we were even on TV! We loved making music together, just like Beth and her friends."

Another book by Anne Miranda

To Market, To Market
Anne Miranda
ILLUSTRATED BY
Janet Stevens

LOG ON Find out more about Anne Miranda at **www.macmillanmh.com**

Author's Purpose

Anne Miranda wanted to show that friends have fun making music. Draw your friends having fun. Write about it.

Comprehension Check

Retell the Story

Use the Retelling Cards
to retell the story.

Retelling Cards

Think and Compare

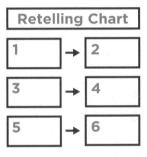

Retelling Chart

1	→	2
3	→	4
5	→	6

1. What do Beth, Ann, Will, and Bud do at the fair?

2. Would you like to join the Kids' Band? Tell why or why not.

3. What other instruments do people play in a band?

4. How is the show in this story like the show in "A Fun Show"?

Shake a Rattle!

What **instruments** do you see here? Shaking **rattles** is a fun way to make **music**.

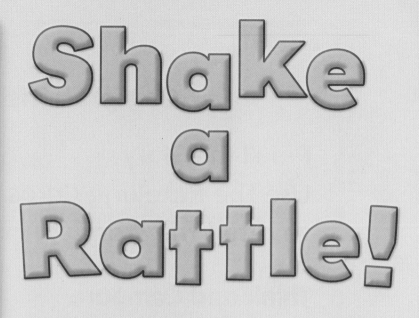

Rattles can be big or little. They can be made of many things. Some have sand in them. Some have beans.

Do you want to make a rattle?
Here's how!

How to Make a Rattle

What You Need

plastic bottle

dried beans

stickers

What to Do

1 Put beans into the bottle.

2 Put fun stickers on.

3 Shake it and have fun!

Can you play the rattle loud?
Can you play it soft? Can you
make up a song?

Connect and Compare

How is a rattle like the instruments the kids made in *The Fun Kids' Band?*

Write About an Animal Band

Leila wrote about a bear in a band.

Billy Bear plays the drum.

The drum goes boom!

Your Turn

Name an animal.

Tell what instrument the animal plays.

Tell what sound it makes.

Writer's Checklist

- ☑ Do special nouns begin with a capital letter?

- ☑ Does my exclamation end with an exclamation mark?

- ☑ Did I use a sound word?

117

Talk About It

What makes you laugh? How do you make other people laugh?

LOG ON Find out more about things that make you laugh at **www.macmillanmh.com**

Let's Laugh

Words to Know

why
late
school
today
away
way

_____

Glen
glad

Read to Find Out

Why is Glen late?

STRATEGY
SKILL

Glen Is Late!

by Tasha Wilson

illustrated by LeUyen Pham

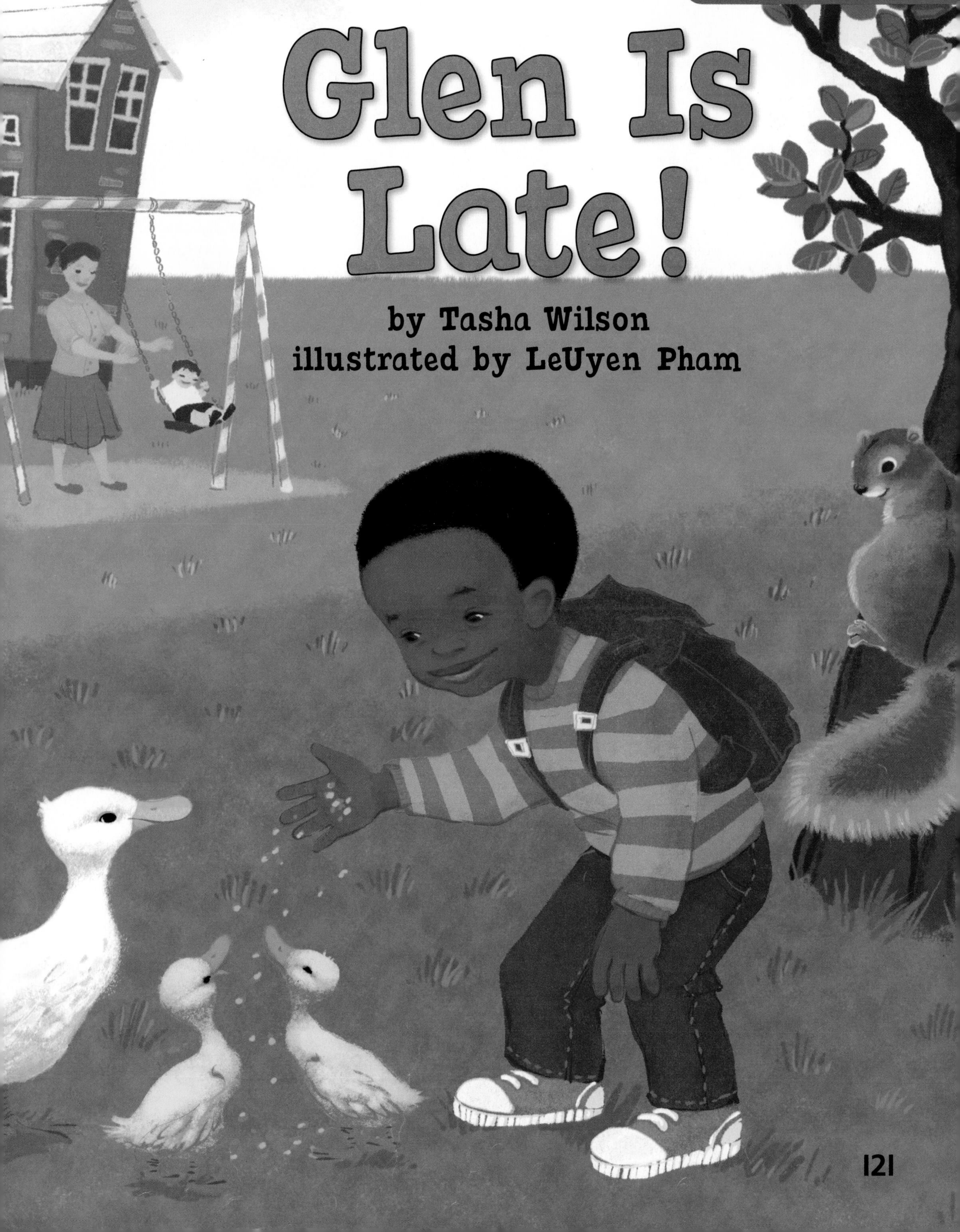

Why is Glen **late** for **school today**?
He wants to see some frogs at play.

The frogs hop up and hop **away**.
They make Glen very late today!

Why is Glen late on his **way** back?
He wants to see the ducks that quack.

The ducks are glad to see him, too.
They are quacking, "We like you!"

Comprehension

Genre

In a **Rhyming Story**, some words end with the same sound.

Visualize

Sequence

As you read, use your **Sequence Chart**.

First

↓

Next

↓

Then

↓

Last

Read to Find Out

What happens to the boy on his way to school?

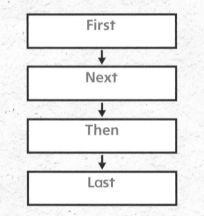

On My Way to School

by Wong Herbert Yee

On my **way** to **school today**,
a pig asks me to come and play.

It's not just a pig.
It's a pig in a wig!
We run for the bus,
just the two of us.

Pig and I run very fast.
We get on the bus at last.
Huff, puff! The bus zips **away**.
Pig makes me **late** for school today!

On my way to school, we pass
a trash truck that ran out of gas.
On top of that truck,
sit two apes and a duck!

The apes and duck hop in the bus.
They sit down with the rest of us.

Slip, flip! The bus zips away.
Apes make me late for school today!

On my way to school, we see
frogs up in a gumdrop tree.

Plip, plop! The gumdrops drop.
Two frogs clip. Two frogs mop.

The frogs hop in the bus.
They sit down with the rest of us.
Hip! Hop! The bus zips away.
Frogs make me late for school today!

Here we go, just one last stop.
The frogs hop in the pond. Plip, plop!

Duck is off to get some gas.
The apes fish and nap in the grass.

Tick, tock! The bus zips away.
It looks like I am late today!

Now, the bus drops me off at school.
I see a crocodile slink out of a pool!

I think it slid under the gate.
And that, Miss Fox, is **why** I am late!

On the Way with Wong Herbert Yee

Wong Herbert Yee says, "No bus picked me up at the corner. I walked a mile to get to school! When I write, I use things that really happened. My imagination fills in the rest. Remember what you see, read, and hear. You may write a funny story, too!"

Other books by Wong Herbert Yee

LOG ON Find out more about Wong Herbert Yee at **www.macmillanmh.com**

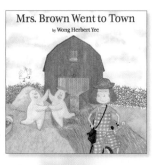

Author's Purpose

Wong Herbert Yee wanted to write a funny story about getting to school. Draw how you get to school. Write about it.

Comprehension Check

Retell the Story

Use the Retelling Cards to retell the story.

Retelling Cards

Think and Compare

1. What makes the boy late first? What makes him late next?

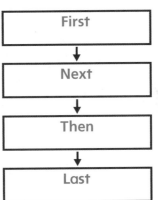

First
↓
Next
↓
Then
↓
Last

2. Have you ever been late for school? Tell what happened.

3. Could this story really happen? Tell why or why not.

4. What makes both the boy in *On My Way to School* and Glen late?

Language Arts

Genre
A **Riddle** is a question with a clever, funny answer.

SKILL

Text Feature
A **Sign** uses words or pictures to give information.

LOG ON
Find out more about riddles at **www.macmillanmh.com**

Take a Riddle Ride

Get Ready to Laugh!

STOP

What do you say to a runaway traffic sign?

Stop, sign!

ENTER

Why did the dog cross the road?

To get to the barking lot.

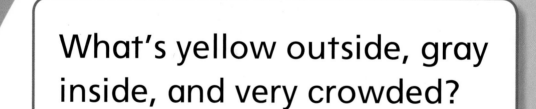

What's yellow outside, gray inside, and very crowded?

A school bus full of elephants.

Connect and Compare

What signs might the children see in *On My Way to School*?

Write a Silly Rhyme

Callie wrote a rhyme about something silly.

On Monday, I saw a cat.

It wore a blue hat!

Your Turn

Imagine something silly.

Write a rhyme about it.

Name the day of the week it happened.

Writer's Checklist

 Do some words rhyme?

 Does the name of the day begin with a capital letter?

 Does each statement end with a special mark?

Lost!

"My frog is lost!" said Jack.

"Let's look for her," said Meg.

Jack looked under the bed.

Meg looked in her pack.

Go on

"What does she like to do?" asked Meg.

"She likes to get wet," said Jack.

They ran to the sink.

There was Frog having a drink!

Directions:
Answer the questions.

I. What did Jack lose?

○   ○   ○

2. Where did Jack look for his pet?

○ in the yard

○ on the bed

○ under the bed

3. What was the pet doing in the sink?

○ having a drink

○ hiding

○ sleeping

Go on ▶

Writing Prompt

Think of a time you lost something.

Did you find it?

Tell about what happened.

Write two or more sentences.

Glossary

What is a Glossary?

A glossary can help you find the meanings of words. The words are listed in alphabetical order. You can look up a word and read it in a sentence. There is a picture to help you.

Sample Entry

Letter

H h

Main Entry

hen

Sentence

A **hen** lays eggs.

Bb

bus

We take the **bus** to school.

Cc

claws

A prairie dog has long **claws**.

Dd

drum

I play the **drum** in the band.

Hh

hen

A **hen** lays eggs.

Ii

instrument

This **instrument** makes a pretty sound.

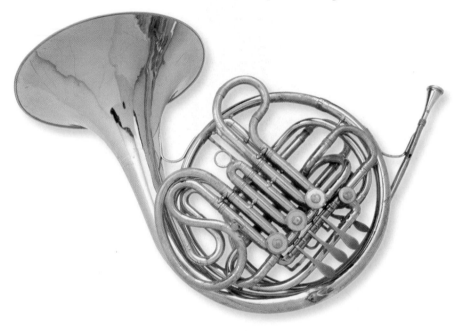

Jj

jug

The **jug** has milk in it.

Ww

wig

I wear a **wig**.

well

Sam got water from a **well**.

Acknowledgments

The publisher gratefully acknowledges permission to reprint the following copyrighted material:

"Over in the Meadow: An Old Counting Rhyme" by Olive A. Wadsworth © 1991, Scholastic Inc., 730 Broadway, NY, NY Reprinted with permission of Scholastic Inc, NY

Book Cover, FIREMAN SMALL by Wong Herbert Yee. Copyright © 1994 by Wong Herbert Yee. Reprinted by permission of Houghton Mifflin Company.

Book Cover, MRS. BROWN WENT TO TOWN by Wong Herbert Yee. Copyright © 2003 by Wong Herbert Yee. Reprinted by permission of Houghton Mifflin.

Book Cover, ROADRUNNER'S DANCE by Rudolfo Anaya, illustrated by David Diaz. Text copyright © 2000 by Rudolfo Anaya. Illustrations copyright © 2000 by /David Diaz. Reprinted by permission of Hyperion Books for Children.

Book Cover, THE LITTLE SCARECROW BOY by Margaret Wise Brown, illustrated by David Diaz. Text copyright © 2005 by Margaret Wise Brown. Illustrations copyright © 2005 by David Diaz. Reprinted by permission of HarperTrophy.

Book Cover, TO MARKET, TO MARKET by Anne Miranda, illustrated by Janet Stevens. Text copyright © 1997 by Anne Miranda. Illustrations copyright © 1997 by Janet Stevens. Reprinted by permission of Harcourt Children's Books.

ILLUSTRATION
Cover Illustration: Lisa Falkenstern

30-35: Krystina Stasiak. 40-45: Dagmar Fehlau. 46-59: David Diaz. 63-66: Tom Leonard. 68: Diane Paterson. 78-79: Rick Nease for TFK. 88-93: Stacy Schuett. 94-109: Lynn Cravath. 116: Diane Paterson. 120-125: LeUyen Pham. 126-141: Wong Herbert Yee. 144-147: Mircea Catusanu. 148: (t),(b) Stacy Schuett; (c) Diane Paterson. 149-151: Stacy Schuett. 154-159: G. Brian Karas.

PHOTOGRAPHY
All Photographs are by Macmillan/McGraw Hill (MMH) except as noted below:

6-7: Steve Bloom Images/Alamy. 7: (tr) G.K. & Vikki Hart/Getty Images, Inc. 8-9: Schafer & Hill/Stone/Getty Images, Inc. 10: (l) Stephen Dalton/Animals Animals/Earth Scenes. 11: Joe McDonald/CORBIS. 12: Robert Lubeck/Animals Animals/Earth Scenes. 13: Tom Brakefield/CORBIS. 14-15: Steve Bloom. 16: Ardea London Ltd. 17: Art Wolfe/Photo Researchers, Inc. 18: Robert Maier/Animals Animals/Earth Scenes. 19: Tom & Pat Leeson/Photo Researchers. 20: Michel & Christine Denis-Huot/Photo Researchers, Inc. 21: Peter Lilja/Taxi/Getty Images, Inc. 22: (l) Tim Flach/Stone/Getty Images, Inc.; 22-23: Joe McDonald/CORBIS. 24: Peter Johnson/CORBIS. 25: Inge Yspeert/CORBIS. 26: Steve Bloom. 27: JM Labat/Peter Arnold, Inc. 28: (tr) Courtesy Jose Ramos; (br) Art Wolfe/Photo Researchers, Inc. 29: Robert Maier/Animals Animals/Earth Scenes. 36: Peter Beck/CORBIS. 37: Marc Romanelli/The Image Bank/Getty Images, Inc. 38-39: Ronnie Kaufman/CORBIS. 39: (tr) Janis Christie/Getty Images, Inc. 60: Courtesy David Diaz. 62: (inset) Photodisc/Getty Images, Inc. 62-63: (bkgd) Adam Gault/Digital Vision Direct; (t) Image 100/Getty Images, Inc. 63: (c) AGStock USA/Alamy; (br) C. Borland/PhotoLink/Getty Images, Inc. 64: (bkgd) c) John Prior Images/Alamy 65: (bkgd) Adam Gault/Digital Vision Direct; (c) JW/Masterfile. 66: (cl) Michael Newman/Photo Edit Inc.; (cl) Stock Food/SuperStock; (t) Larry Lefever/Grant Heilman Photography. 67: (c) Brand X Pictures/Alamy. 68: Tony Anderson/Taxi/Getty Images, Inc. 69: Michael Newman/Photo Edit Inc. 70-71: Konrad Wothe/Minden Pictures. 72: (t) Don Farrall/Photodisc/Getty Images, Inc.; (c) Steve Bronstein/The Image Bank/Getty Images, Inc. 73: (t) Daniel L. Geiger/SNAP/Alamy; (inset) Daniel L. Geiger/SNAP/Alamy. 74-75: (bkgd) Leonard Rue Enterprises/Animals Animals. 75: (inset) Gloria H. Chomica/Masterfile. 76: (bkgd) Jim Brandenburg/Minden Pictures; (inset) D. Robert & Lorri Franz/CORBIS. 77: (tl) Tom and Pat Leeson; (r) Donald Mammoser/Bruce Coleman Inc. 80-81: David Boag/Alamy. 82: CORBIS/Punchstock. 83: (tl) CORBIS/Punchstock; (tr) Andrew Taylor/Alamy; (tc) Craig Tuttle/CORBIS; (bl) Photolink/Getty Images, Inc.; (bc) Neil Homes/Garden Picture Library/Alamy; (br) Photodisc/Getty Images, Inc. 84: Robin Davies/Taxi/Getty Images, Inc. 85: (c) Dian Lofton for TFK; (cr) C Squared Studios/Photodisc/Getty Images, Inc.; (br) C Squared Studios/Photodisc/Getty Images, Inc. 86-87: Bob Daemmrich/The Image Works, Inc. 87: (tr) Steve Cole/Getty Images, Inc. 114: (bl) David Young-Wolff/Photo Edit Inc.; (bc) allOver Photography/Alamy; (br) Royalty-Free/CORBIS; (cr) Canadian Museum of Civilization/CORBIS; (t),(bl) Ken Karp. 115: (t) AP-Wide World Photos; (br) Dynamic Graphics Group/Creatas/Alamy; (tl),(tr) Ken Karp. 118-119: Tim Fitzharris/Masterfile. 119: (tr) Doug Menuez/Getty Images, Inc. 142: Courtesy Wong Herbert Yee. 144: Photodisc/Getty Images, Inc. 145: Joseph Sohm/Alamy. 146: Royalty-Free/CORBIS. 147: Stockdisc/Picture Quest. 150: (l) PhotoDisc/Getty Images, Inc.; (r) Eyewire/Getty Images, Inc.; (c) Dan Suzio/Photo Researchers, Inc. 155: Gary Buss/Taxi/Getty Images, Inc. 156: (t) Gary Buss/Taxi/Getty Images, Inc. 157: Robert Maier/Animals Animals. 158: C Squared Studios/Getty Images, Inc. 159: Joseph Sohm; ChromoSohm Inc./CORBIS